# TRYTHIS!
# Sewing

## Stephanie Turnbull

A+
**Smart Apple Media**

Published by Smart Apple Media, an imprint of Black Rabbit Books
P.O. Box 3263, Mankato, Minnesota, 56002
www.blackrabbitbooks.com

Printed in the United States of America, at Corporate Graphics
in North Mankato, Minnesota.

Designed and illustrated by Guy Callaby
Edited by Mary-Jane Wilkins

Cataloging-in-Publication Data is available from the Library of Congress

ISBN 978-1-62588-375-9

Photo acknowledgements
t = top, b = bottom, c = center, l = left, r = right
page 1 djem/Shutterstock; 3 Mim Waller; 4, 5, OlgaNik;
6 Louella938/both Shutterstock; 9, 11, 13, 15, 17, 19, 21
Mim Waller; 22 Radu Razvan; 23 oldnetz/both Shutterstock
Cover top right Jupiterimages, main iimage tuja66/both Thinkstock

DAD0062b
012016
9 8 7 6 5 4 3

# Contents

# Why try sewing?

**Sewing is a fantastic hobby.
Here are a few reasons to try it!**

## 1 It's easy to learn.

Sewing doesn't have to be hard. You can create impressive toys, bags, and decorations using just a few very simple stitches.

## 2 You don't need expensive supplies.

Start with a **needle**, **thread**, and fabric to stitch. It's fun to use **felt**, which is easy to cut and sew. A few extras such as buttons and beads may come in handy.

*Simple sewing kits often contain needles, pins, thread, and other useful supplies.*

**3 It makes a great gift.**
Handmade presents are much more special than bought ones. Try making sewn cushions, bookmarks, and even cards for your friends and family. How about stitching their name on a T-shirt?

Now test out the brilliant projects in this book and see for yourself how much fun sewing can be. Look out for the helpful tips and extra ideas.

**4 It looks amazing!**
Brighten up your bedroom with cool sewn creations. They look so good, no one will ever believe how easy they were to make!

# Simple stitching

**First, learn to thread a needle and tie a knot. Then you can start stitching!**

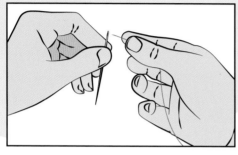

**1** *Find a needle and cut a long length of thread. Feed the thread through the needle's eye (hole). If it's too small, use a needle with a bigger eye.*

**2** *Pull the thread through the hole, so it doesn't fall out. Now wrap the end of the thread twice around your index finger.*

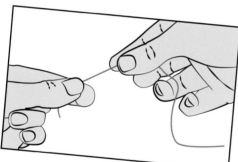

**3** *Use your thumb to roll the loop slowly off your finger.*

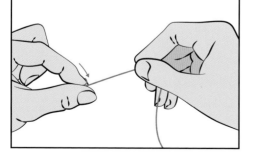

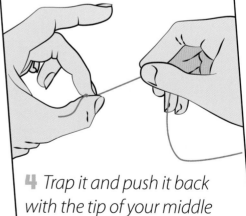

**4** *Trap it and push it back with the tip of your middle finger so it makes a knot.*

**5** *Push your needle up through a piece of fabric, so the knot is on the back. Now push the needle back down, and up again. You've made your first stitch!*

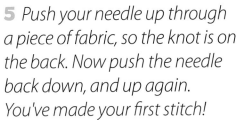

**6** *Carry on in the same way to make a line of stitches. Try to keep them the same size.*

**7** *To finish, push the needle to the back of the fabric. Feed it through the last stitch…*

*… then pass the needle through the loop you just made. Pull it tight to make a knot. Cut off the thread.*

*Don't pull your stitches too tight or the fabric will bunch up.*

### Now try this
*Make a bookmark by sewing lines down a strip of felt. Create a wiggly effect by threading a different color thread in and out of stitches (see photo, page 2).*

# Tic tac toe board

**This felt board game is simple to make and fun to play.**

**1** Cut a 6-inch (15-cm) square of felt. Use a ruler to measure two vertical lines and two horizontal lines, each 2 inches (5 cm) apart, then mark them with pins.

Choose a color that stands out well. Tie a knot.

**2** Thread a needle with thick thread (as on page 6). **Tapestry thread** works well.

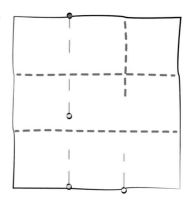

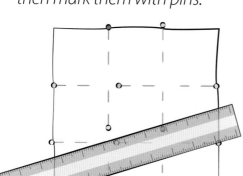

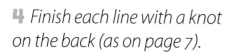

**3** Now sew along the lines on the felt. Remove each pin as you come to it.

**4** Finish each line with a knot on the back (as on page 7).

**5** Now cut ten short strips of felt. Sew them together in pairs to make crosses.

**6** Cut five felt circles and decorate them with extra stitches. You're ready to play!

## Now try this

Try **backstitch**. Make an ordinary stitch, then push the needle down through the felt at the end of the first stitch to create two joined stitches with no gap. Come up again a space away from the new stitch, then do the same again.

**Ordinary stitches look like this.**

**Backstitches loop back each time.**

Pins and needles are sharp! Stick them in **pin cushions** when you aren't using them.

# Easy decorations

**Create fantastic hanging decorations using felt shapes and just a small amount of sewing.**

**1** *Decide on a few shapes and cut one of each from cardstock.*

**2** *Use these as templates to draw around on felt. Cut out lots of shapes.*

**3** *Lay the shapes in a line. Thread a needle with thick thread and sew them together with big stitches to make a long string.*

**Leave a gap between each shape.**

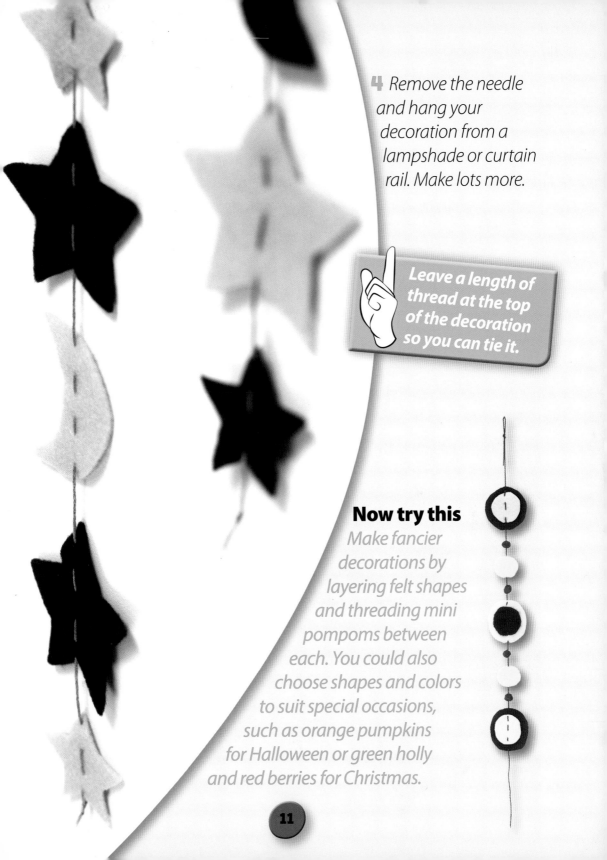

**4** Remove the needle and hang your decoration from a lampshade or curtain rail. Make lots more.

Leave a length of thread at the top of the decoration so you can tie it.

**Now try this**

Make fancier decorations by layering felt shapes and threading mini pompoms between each. You could also choose shapes and colors to suit special occasions, such as orange pumpkins for Halloween or green holly and red berries for Christmas.

# Felt friends

**Try making a brilliant felt bear using this straightforward design.**

1 Draw an oval, about 3 inches (8 cm) long, on cardstock and cut it out. This is your body pattern. Draw around it twice on brown felt, then cut out the shapes.

2 Cut two ear shapes and four paws from brown felt, plus a small circle of white felt.

Turn over felt shapes to hide any pen marks from drawing around the templates.

3 Sew the white circle onto one of the body ovals. Use small, neat stitches in white thread.

4 Now sew lots of little black stitches to make eyes, a nose, and a mouth.

**5** Put the two body ovals together and sew along the edges with brown thread. When you come to places where ears or paws go, sandwich them between the ovals and stitch them, too.

Don't go all the way around—leave a gap.

**6** Push a little **stuffing** or cotton inside, then finish sewing around the edge.

## Now try this

Use similar shapes to make pigs, frogs, fish, pandas, birds, and more. Use your imagination!

# Drawstring bags

**Use this stylish bag as a money pouch, a gift bag, or to store precious things in.**

**1** *Cut a rectangle of felt and fold it double.*

**The size depends on how big you want your bag to be.**

**2** *Sew up each long side. Backstitching (see page 9) is great for this as it doesn't leave big gaps.*

**3** *Turn the bag inside out. Thread a needle with thick, bright thread. Don't tie a knot.*

**4** *Make a big stitch across one side of the bag, near the top. Leave a long end of thread dangling.*

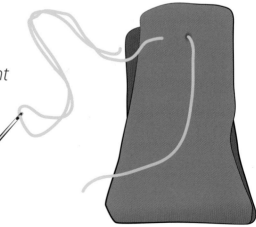

**5** *Stitch around the bag. Remove the needle and cut the two ends of thread to the same length. Pull to tighten them, and tie in a bow.*

**Don't fasten thread in a knot or it could be tricky to untie.**

## Now try this

*Give your bag extra style by adding beads to the ends of the thread. Tie knots to keep them in place.*

# Clever cushions

## Why not transform an old T-shirt into a cool cushion for your bedroom?

**1** *Turn a T-shirt inside out. Rule a line across it, just below the arms, or mark out a line with pins.*

**2** *Sew across the line with ordinary stitches or backstitch. Go through both layers.*

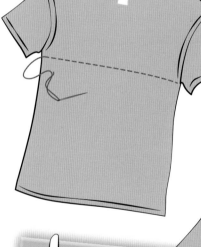

**3** *Cut away the top of the T-shirt, about ½ inch (1 cm) above the sewn line.*

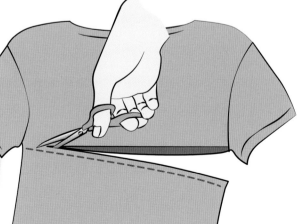

Keep the top of the T-shirt in case you need it for other sewing projects!

*Choose T-shirts with colors and patterns that suit your room.*

**4** Turn the T-shirt the right side out and fill it with pillow stuffing or old towels and socks.

**5** Stitch up the opening. Sew along the **seams** so your stitches don't show.

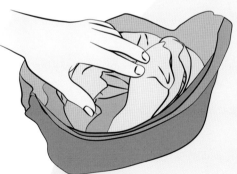

## Now try this

*Try sewing felt shapes or buttons onto your cushion as decoration. Do this before you stuff it and sew it up.*

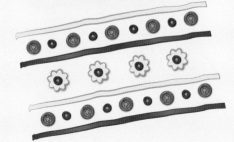

# Hooded towel

**This cozy hooded towel is amazingly easy to sew. You need one big bath towel and a matching hand towel.**

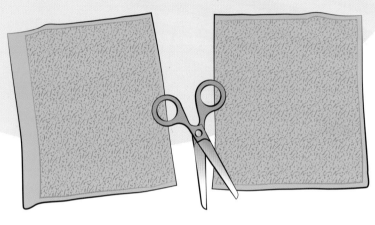

**hand towel**

**1** *Cut the hand towel in half and put one half aside.*

**2** *Lay the bath towel on the floor, underside up. Place the hand towel half at the top, in the middle, underside up. Pin the edges together.*

**3** *Stitch the edges together.*

Use thread that matches the towel color.

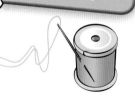

**bath towel**

**4** *Turn over the towels and fold them in half, like this. Pin the cut end of the hand towel together about 1 inch (2.5 cm) from the top. Sew it up.*

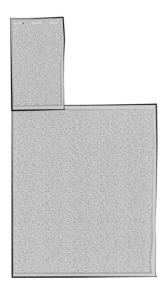

**5** *Turn the hood the right way out.*

## Now try this

*Use the other half of the hand towel to make a bath **mitt**. Sketch a mitt shape on paper, then use it as a pattern to cut two shapes from the towel. Sew them together with the undersides facing outward, then turn the right way out.*

# Sewn star bursts

**Sewing on cardstock can create fantastic effects.**

**1** *Cut a piece of thick cardstock. Draw around something circular.*

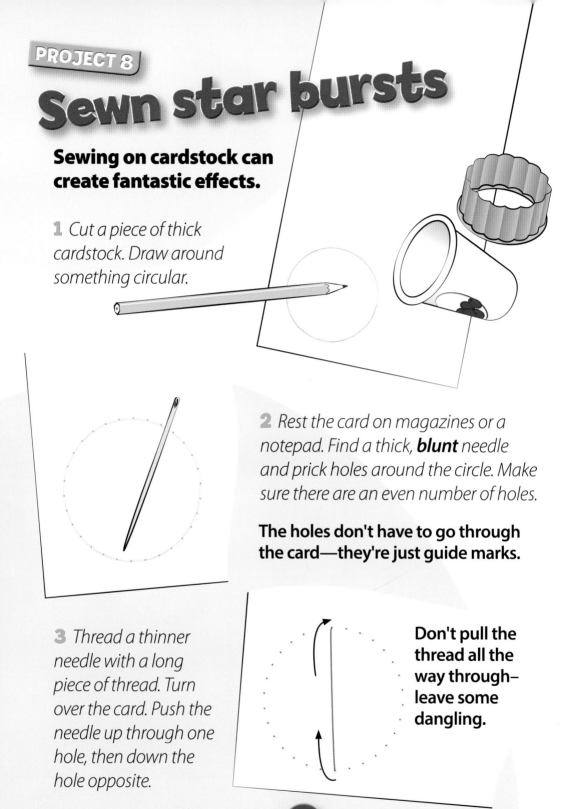

**2** *Rest the card on magazines or a notepad. Find a thick, **blunt** needle and prick holes around the circle. Make sure there are an even number of holes.*

**The holes don't have to go through the card—they're just guide marks.**

**3** *Thread a thinner needle with a long piece of thread. Turn over the card. Push the needle up through one hole, then down the hole opposite.*

**Don't pull the thread all the way through–leave some dangling.**

**4** Come up at the hole to the left of the one you first came up through, and go down the one to the right of the second.

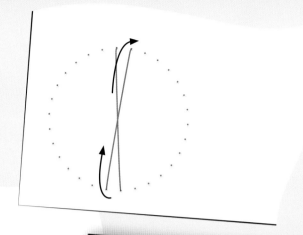

**5** Keep going like this until you've been through each hole. Cut the thread at the back and tape down the ends.

**6** Draw more circles and build up a pattern of stylish star bursts.

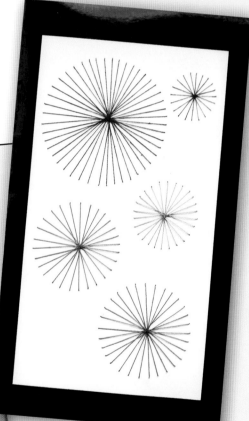

Start with two holes directly opposite each other. Count the holes to make sure there are the same number on each side.

## Now try this
*Mount your design on a bigger piece of card, or make it into a greeting card.*

# Glossary

**backstitch**
A style of stitching in which you keep going back to fill in gaps between stitches. This creates a neat, unbroken line of sewing.

**blunt**
Not sharp at the end. The bluntest needles are big, thick darning needles.

**felt**
Soft fabric made from matted, pressed wool. Felt comes in different colors and doesn't fray (unravel) when cut into shapes.

**mitt**
Short for mitten; a glove without fingers.

**mount**
To fix something in place on a background (such as a piece of thick card) to display it.

**needle**
A pointed, slim piece of metal with a hole at one end (called an eye). Needles vary in size, so choose one that suits the material you're sewing and the thickness of your thread. The thinner the fabric, the thinner your needle can be.

**pin cushion**
A soft, fabric-covered ball or other shape, used to stick pins and needles in to keep them safe.

### seam
The join where two pieces of fabric are sewn together.

### stuffing
Soft, fluffy material that you can buy in packs or take out from old pillows or soft toys.

### tapestry thread
A special, thick type of thread. Tapestry thread comes in lots of colors and is great when you want your stitches to stand out.

### thread
A long, thin strand of cotton. Thread comes in lots of different colors and thicknesses, so choose one that suits your material and use a needle with an eye (hole) big enough to feed the thread through. Remember to tie a knot at the end before you start to sew.

**www.holiday-crafts-and-creations.com/craft-tips.html**
Learn basic stitches using these clear instructions and photos.

**www.bhg.com/crafts/kids/rainy-day/kids-felt-crafts**
Practice your sewing skills with fun felt crafts.

**tlc.howstuffworks.com/family/sewing-crafts.htm**
Test out some great sewing projects.

# Index